MY SPEECH WORKBOOK

NAME:

Year:

PLEASE NOTE: This Student Workbook is meant to be used in conjunction with the "Public Speaking for Kids – Level 1 Teaching Guide." If you are not taking this class with an instructor, you will need to purchase a copy. www.bigbrainbuzz.com

All Rights Reserved. No portion of this publication may be reproduced by any means, including duplicating, photocopying, electronic, mechanical, recording, the World Wide Web, e-mail, or otherwise, without written permission from the publisher.

Copyright © November 2019 by Big Brain Buzz. Independently Published.

Publisher:

Big Brain Buzz
Darlington, WI 53530

Public Speaking for Kids Level 1 Teaching Manual is part of the Public Speaking for Kids Program. For more books and resources in this series, go to www.bigbrainbuzz.com.

Words of Praise for
Public Speaking for Kids – Level One

"Why is Speech class an elective in education, rather than a requirement? We ought to make public speaking a priority in our children's educations! Ultimately, these are the skills they are going to have for the rest of their lives! "Public Speaking for Kids" is the perfect solution to the problem and is easy to implement in schools, homeschool communities, co-ops, speech clubs, and even at home. This practical, "how-to" guide (when combined with the Student Workbook) grabs both the instructor and the student's attention to make learning engaging and fun. I have been teaching and coaching competitive Speech and Debate for over a decade. People are always asking me how to get started or where to start when they have younger students, not quite competitive age. I am super excited that I will be able to point teachers, homeschool parents, co-op leaders, and club coaches to the 'Public Speaking for Kids' series." – *Heather Nuemann, Lasting Impact   www.lastingimpact.info*

"We have loved this curriculum so far! The best part is how easy it is to use and how well-organized each week is. I like how each week a new presentation skill is added. The cue picture that goes along with each new skill makes incorporating that skill into the speech easy. My kids like how the outline pages provide just the right amount of guidance while keeping it simple." - *Sarah M., Parent*

"Pull-out and go! Very user-friendly! No need to struggle with what to teach next! Excellent check-off list! The kids love it! They can't wait to present! I have had students tell me on Sunday that they can't wait to give their speech on Friday! They beg to do their presentations! The curriculum helps develop excellent speakers and presenters when they are young! It takes so little time and the rewards are tremendous!" - *Michelle M., Public Speaking Co-op Instructor*

"This speech curriculum has been an excellent resource for our family. It is extremely easy to use. My children's ability to create and present speeches has greatly improved." – *Whitney M., Parent*

Welcome Parent!

There is no skill more needed among today's generation than the art of communication. Regardless of the career path chosen by your students, speaking eloquently and confidently will be a cornerstone in their life.

This class will take your students on a journey to understand, develop, and refine their speaking skills. Each week, your students will have the opportunity to build on an earlier skill using this resource as a guide.

*This Student Workbook is designed to be used in conjunction with the Public Speaking for Kids – Level 1 Teaching Guide. If you are not taking the class with an instructor, you will need to purchase a copy to accompany this resource.

Join the "Big Brain Buzz – Public Speaking for Kids Private Facebook Group" to share your student's speeches and get feeback from the author and other community members!

How You Can Help Your Student

- Encourage them to practice daily
- Follow the suggested schedule below:

SUGGESTED AT-HOME SCHEDULE

DAY ONE:	Read the scorecard from the last class time to see what you did well, and what you can improve upon. Use the Roadmap to create the speech. Present the speech to someone to see if things need added, modified, or taken out.
DAY TWO:	Convert the Roadmap to the Outline (introduced in week 4). Practice making all of your points using the outline provided rather than reading word for word.
DAY THREE:	Practice your speech again and focus on your delivery – is the speech exciting, engaging, interesting? What can you add to it to make it better?
DAY FOUR:	Perfect your speech. Present it multiple times to make sure you are confident. Make sure your audience is engaged and is able to identify all of your main points.
DAY FIVE:	Presentation in front of class & new instruction.
Speech to Prepare for Next Class:	This section provides a quick-glance at the assigned speech topic for the following week (student homework) ***Speech topics on the following pages are suggested according to the style of speech taught in class each week. For additional / optional speech titles by week, as well as free worksheets & downloads, visit www.bigbrainbuzz.com/PublicSpeakingFreebies

YEAR AT A GLANCE

	Creation Skill	Delivery Skill	TEACHING PROP	Suggested In Class Speech*	Speech Type	Suggested Homework Topic*
Week 1	Talk about 2 parts of speech – building & performing Informative Speeches	NEW: 3 second rule	Stoplight	All About Me	Impromptu	Favorite & Least Favorite Foods & why
Week 2	INTRODUCE: Organization: – 3 things	REVIEW: 3 second rule	Stoplight, Three Big Ideas (1,2,3)	Favorite & Least Favorite Foods & why	Informative	Favorite Toy/game
Week 3	REVIEW: Organization: – 3 things NEW: Outlines	NEW: Voice: Volume	Stoplight, & Three Big Ideas (123) poster, & Ear sticks	Favorite Toy/Game	Informative	Favorite Trip/thing to do in the summer
Week 4	REVIEW: Organization: – 3 things Outlines	NEW: Poise: Body Language	Ear, Tree, & snake sticks	Favorite Trip/thing to do in the summer	Informative	An Animal & its habitat
Week 5	NEW: Organization: Hook	REVIEW: Poise: Body Language	Ear, Tree, & Snake sticks, Fish Hook	An Animal & its habitat	Informative	Interesting Information About A Different Country
Week 6	REVIEW: Organization: – 3 things Hook	NEW: Eye Contact NEW: Memorization	Ear & Eye sticks	Interesting Information About A Different Country	Informative	Your Favorite book or Movie
Week 7	NEW: Organization: Closing	REVIEW: Eye Contact & Memorization	Eye, Door	Your Favorite book or Movie	Informative	A Career (Firefighter, Police, Ballerina, etc)
Week 8	REVIEW: Organization : Closing	NEW: Speed: Pace & Clarity	Walking Shoe sticks	A Career (Firefighter, Police, Ballerina, etc)	Informative	Which Season of the Year You Love the Most or Favorite Subjects in School

	Creation Skill	Delivery Skill	TEACHING PROP	Suggested In Class Speech*	Speech Type	Suggested Homework Topic*
Week 9	REVIEW: Organization : Closing NEW: Persuasive Speeches	REVIEW: Voice & Speed	"Walking Shoes" Sticks	Which Season of the Year You Love the Most or Favorite Subjects in School	Persuasive	You should eat these three foods…
Week 10	NEW: Organization : – 3 things + 3 things	REVIEW: Voice Speed Eye Contact Poise	Submarine Poster	You should eat these three foods…	Persuasive	Parents should….get a pet/game, go on a vacation
Week 11	REVIEW: Organization : – 3 things + 3 things	REVIEW: Voice Speed Eye Contact Poise	$ Dollar bills	Parents should….get a pet/game, go on a vacation	Persuasive	Commercial: Every Parent should buy this for their kid…
Week 12	REVIEW: Organization : – 3 things + 3 things	REVIEW: Voice Speed Eye Contact Poise	$ Dollar bills	Commercial: Every Parent should buy this for their kid…	Persuasive	Your Choice!
Week 13	REVIEW: Organization : – 3 things + 3 things	REVIEW: Voice Speed Eye Contact Poise	Impromptu Slips, All popsicle stick items, All posters	2 minute impromptu trying to use all skills.	Impromptu	Impromptu
Week 14	NEW: Visual Aids / Using Props	REVIEW	Impromptu Slips, Visual Aid from home	Impromptu	Impromptu	Show & Tell
Week 15	REVIEW: Visual Aids / Using Props	REVIEW	Props for teacher demonstration	Show & Tell	Demonstration w/ Visual Aids	Demonstration w/ visual Aids
Week 16	How to select a Poem or Short Story	NEW: Voice: Changing Voices or Sounds	Penguin Pirate poster	Demonstration "How this works" or "How to"	Demonstration w/ Visual Aids	Poetry or Reading or Short Story

	Creation Skill	Delivery Skill	TEACHING PROP	Suggested In Class Speech*	Speech Type	Suggested Homework Topic*
Week 17	How to select a Poem or Short Story	NEW: Gestures: Add Movement	Penguin Pirate & Red Bird	Poetry or Reading	Dramatic Interpretive	Practice the same Poetry/Reading or Short Story
Week 18	REVIEW: Importance of Memorization	REVIEW: Gestures: Add Movement	Memory Man Poster	Poetry or Reading	Dramatic Interpretive	Memorize & Perfect your Poetry/Reading or Short Story
Week 19	Ideas for Famous Speeches & Examples	NEW: Speed: Changing tempo	Racecar	Poetry or Reading	Dramatic Interpretive	Practice a portion of a Famous Speech
Week 20	NEW: Notecards	REVIEW: Speed: Changing tempo	Race Car	Famous Speeches	Dramatic Interpretive	Convert your Famous Speech to an Outline or Notecards
Week 21	REVIEW: Notecards NEW: Time Limit	NEW: Voice: Volume Changes for Emphasis	Eyeball sticks & Megaphone	Famous Speeches	Dramatic Interpretive	Memorize your Famous Speech
Week 22	REVIEW: Memorization	REVIEW: Gestures	Megaphone & Red Bird	Famous Speeches	Dramatic Interpretive	Continue Working on your Famous Speech
Week 23	NEW: Appearance: Dressing for your speech	REVIEW Gestures	Fancy Lion	Famous Speeches	Dramatic Interpretive	Perfect Your Famous Speech
Week 24	REVIEW: Appearance	Famous Speeches		Famous Speech	Dramatic Interpretive	

Glossary of Terms & Tips

Clarity – Enunciation becomes critical in public speaking. We should strive to clearly communicate each word

Closing – A creative ending. Many times, it should relate back to your hook at the beginning.

Eye contact – Make each member of the audience feel as if you are speaking to them by making eye contact.

Gestures – Using your physical body to portray a character or scene. You may also use gestures to emphasize various points in your speech.

Hook – An interesting introduction - The audience is excited to hear our speech when we start with a quote, interesting fact, a story, or an attention-grabbing statement.

Impromptu – A speech in which the presenter has very little time to prepare. These can sometimes be called "limited prep".

Informative – A speech that communicates facts or opinion about a topic.

Interpretive – A speech where the presenter becomes part of the story through acting and characterization.

Pace/Tempo – the rate at which you speak.

Persuasive – A type of speech that convinces someone to think or act in a certain way.

Poise – The way you position your body while speaking. You should stand tall and confident.

Sub-topics – these are three lesser topics that refer back to one of your "Three Big Ideas"

"Three Big Ideas" - *When you are speaking on a topic, you want to try to come up with at least three main points to make.*

"Three Second Rule" – Wait Three full seconds before starting your speech to make sure the audience is ready to listen.

Visual aids/props – These could be posters, graphs, props, gadgets, or any other physical tool you use to help communicate your ideas.

Volume – Speak at a level that is comfortable for all members of the audience to listen to.

Week 1 - Scorecard

I FELT......

About My Speech Today

I Used the 3-Second Rule:

YES   NO

Week 2 - RoadMap

NEW SKILL: Wait for the audience to be ready before you start. Slowly count to three inside your head before you begin.

Speech Topic:

My Favorite "_____"

My Favorite "_____" are:
_____
_____

Because.....
_____
_____
_____
_____

I Don't Really Like:
_____
_____

Because.....
_____
_____
_____

I practiced reciting my speech: ☐ ☐ ☐ ☐ ☐ ☐ ☐

Week 2 - Scorecard

I FELT......

About My Speech Today

I Used the 3-Second Rule:

YES   NO

Week 3 - RoadMap

New Skill: 123
Think of three Big Ideas to share with your audience!

Speech Topic:
My Favorite _____

🚦 My Favorite _____ :

1   2   3

1 I Like _____ Because...

_____

_____

2 I Like _____ Because...

_____

_____

3 I Like _____ Because...

_____

_____

1   2   3

I practiced reciting My Speech: ☐ ☐ ☐ ☐ ☐ ☐ ☐

Week 3 - Scorecard

I FELT......

About My Speech Today

I Used the 3-Second Rule:	My Speech Had Three Big Ideas:
 YES / NO	 YES / NO

Week 4 - RoadMap

New Skill: Volume: Speak loud enough so everyone can hear your pleasant voice.

Speech Topic: _____

My Favorite _____

My Favorite _____ :

1   **2**   **3**

1 I Like _____ Because...

_____

_____

2 I Like _____ Because...

_____

_____

3 I Like _____ Because...

_____

_____

1   **2**   **3**

I practiced reciting My Speech: ☐ ☐ ☐ ☐ ☐ ☐ ☐

Week 4 - Outline

My Favorite _____ :

1   **2**   **3**

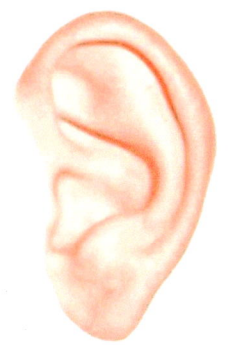

1.
   Because...

2.
   Because...

Volume:
Speak loud
enough so
everyone can
hear your
pleasant
voice.

3.
   Because...

I practiced reciting my speech: ☐ ☐ ☐ ☐ ☐ ☐ ☐

Week 4 - Scorecard

I FELT......

About My Speech Today

Everyone in the room heard my Speech Clearly

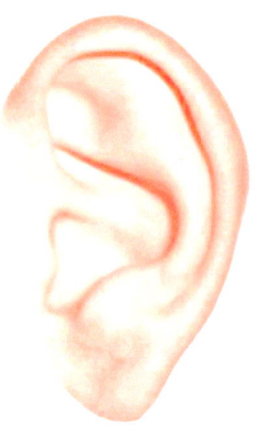

YES   NO

I Used the 3-Second Rule:

 YES

NO

My Speech Had Three Big Ideas:

 YES

NO

Week 5 - RoadMap

NEW SKILL: <u>Poise – Body Language:</u> Stand tall and don't fidget! No rocking, twisting or flipping hair, slouching, etc. Be bold and confident!

I practiced reciting my speech: ☐ ☐ ☐ ☐ ☐ ☐ ☐

Week 5 - Outline

"_____"

1   2   3

1.

Poise: Stand tall and don't fidget!

2.

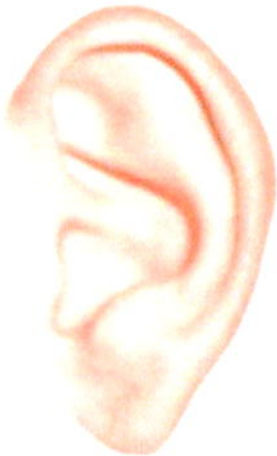

Volume: Make sure everyone in the room can hear you.

3.

1   2   3

I practiced reciting my speech: ☐ ☐ ☐ ☐ ☐ ☐ ☐

Week 5 - Scorecard

Speech Writing Skills

 My Speech Had Three Big Ideas: YES   NO

Speech Delivery Skills

 I Used the 3-Second Rule: YES   NO

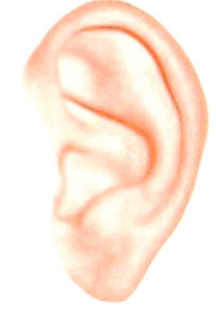 Everyone in the room heard My Speech Clearly: YES   NO

 I Stood Tall & Didn't Fidget: YES   NO

Week 6 - RoadMap

New Skill: <u>Organization: Add a Hook</u> The audience is excited to hear my speech when I start with a quote, interesting fact, a story, or an attention-grabbing statement.

🚦 "_____"

1   2   3

1 _____

_____

2 _____

_____

3 _____

_____

1   2   3

I practiced reciting my speech: ☐ ☐ ☐ ☐ ☐ ☐

Week 6 - Outline

"_____"

1.

2.

3.

Poise: Stand tall and don't fidget!

Volume: Make sure everyone in the room can hear you.

I practiced My Speech: ☐ ☐ ☐ ☐ ☐ ☐ ☐

Week 6 - Scorecard

Speech Writing Skills

 My Speech Began With a Hook: YES   NO

 My Speech Had Three Big Ideas: YES   NO

Speech Delivery Skills

 I Used the 3-Second Rule: YES   NO

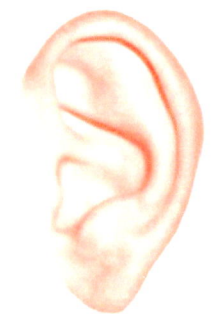 Everyone in the Room Heard My Speech Clearly: YES   NO

 I Stood Tall & Didn't Fidget: YES   NO

Week 7 - RoadMap

New Skill: Eye Contact: Be sure to look your audience in the eye. Look up from your outline or notes frequently.

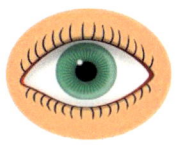
" _____ "

1 2 3

1

2

3

1 2 3

I practiced reciting my speech: ☐ ☐ ☐ ☐ ☐ ☐ ☐

Week 7 - Outline

"_____"

       1   **2**   **3**

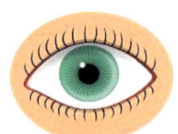

Eye Contact: Look your audience in the eye.

1.

2.

Poise: Stand tall and don't fidget!

3.

       1   **2**   **3**

I practiced reciting my speech: ☐ ☐ ☐ ☐ ☐ ☐ ☐

Week 7 - Scorecard

Speech Writing Skills

 My Speech Began With a Hook: YES   NO

 My Speech Had Three Big Ideas: YES   NO

Speech Delivery Skills

 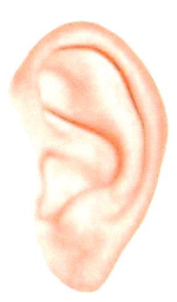  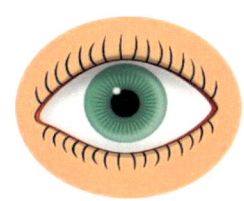

Circle the Items You Included in Your Speech.

Underline the Items you Forgot.

Week 8 - RoadMap

 **NeW SKiLL:** <u>Organization - Closing:</u> Help the audience know you are ending your speech by including a creative and clear ending.

🚦 "_____"

1   **2**   **3**

1 _____
_____
_____

2 _____
_____
_____

3 _____
_____
_____

1   **2**   **3**

I practiced reciting My Speech: ☐ ☐ ☐ ☐ ☐ ☐ ☐

Week 8 - Outline

_____

       1   2   3

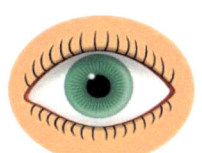

Eye Contact: Look your audience in the eye.

1.

2.

Poise: Stand tall and don't fidget!

3.

       1   2   3

I practiced reciting my speech: ☐ ☐ ☐ ☐ ☐ ☐ ☐

Week 8 - Scorecard

Speech Writing Skills

Speech Delivery Skills

 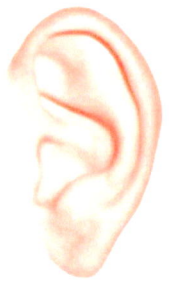  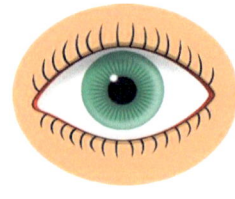

Circle the items you included in your speech.

Underline the items you forgot.

Week 9 – RoadMap

 **NeW SKiLL:** **Speed:** My words should be spoken at a walking pace. We don't race to the end, or wait in silence. These "shoes" remind me to speak at a comfortable

"_____"

I practiced reciting My Speech: ☐ ☐ ☐ ☐ ☐ ☐ ☐

Week 9 - Outline

"_____"

1   **2**   **3**

1.

Speed: Speak at a "walking pace".

2.

Eye Contact: Look your audience in the eye

3.

1   **2**   **3**

I practiced reciting my speech: ☐ ☐ ☐ ☐ ☐ ☐ ☐

Week 9 - Scorecard

Speech Writing Skills

Speech Delivery Skills

 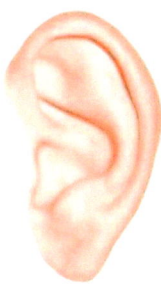  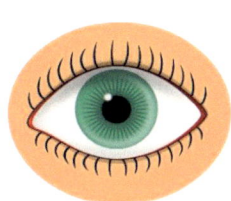 

Circle the items you included in your speech.

Underline the items you forgot.

Week 10 - Roadmap

NEW STYLE: <u>Persuasive Speeches:</u> Use your words to convince, direct, or guide the audience into a belief or an action. You will need to think about who your audience is, and what things might appeal to them.

🚦 "_____"

1.   2.   3.

1.

2.

3.

1.   2.   3.

I practiced reciting my speech: ☐ ☐ ☐ ☐ ☐ ☐ ☐

Week 10 - Outline

_____

1 **2** **3**

1.

Speed: Speak at a "walking pace".

2.

Eye Contact: Look your audience in the eye.

3.

1 **2** **3**

I practiced reciting my speech: ☐ ☐ ☐ ☐ ☐ ☐ ☐

Week 10 - Scorecard

Speech Writing Skills

Speech Delivery Skills

 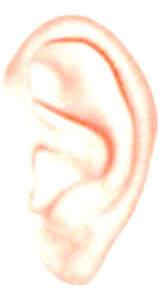  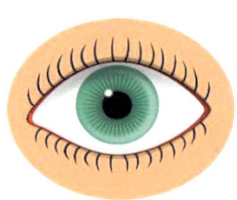 

Circle **THREE** skills you did well.

Underline **TWO** items to work on next week.

Week 11 - RoadMap

NEW SKILL: <u>Three Sub-topics:</u> You are getting good at talking about three main topics. We will now add sub-topics. Under each main topic, describe three things related to that topic!

"_____"

1 2 3

1

1
2
3

2

1
2
3

3

1
2
3

1 2 3

I practiced reciting My Speech: ☐ ☐ ☐ ☐ ☐ ☐ ☐

Week 11 - Outline

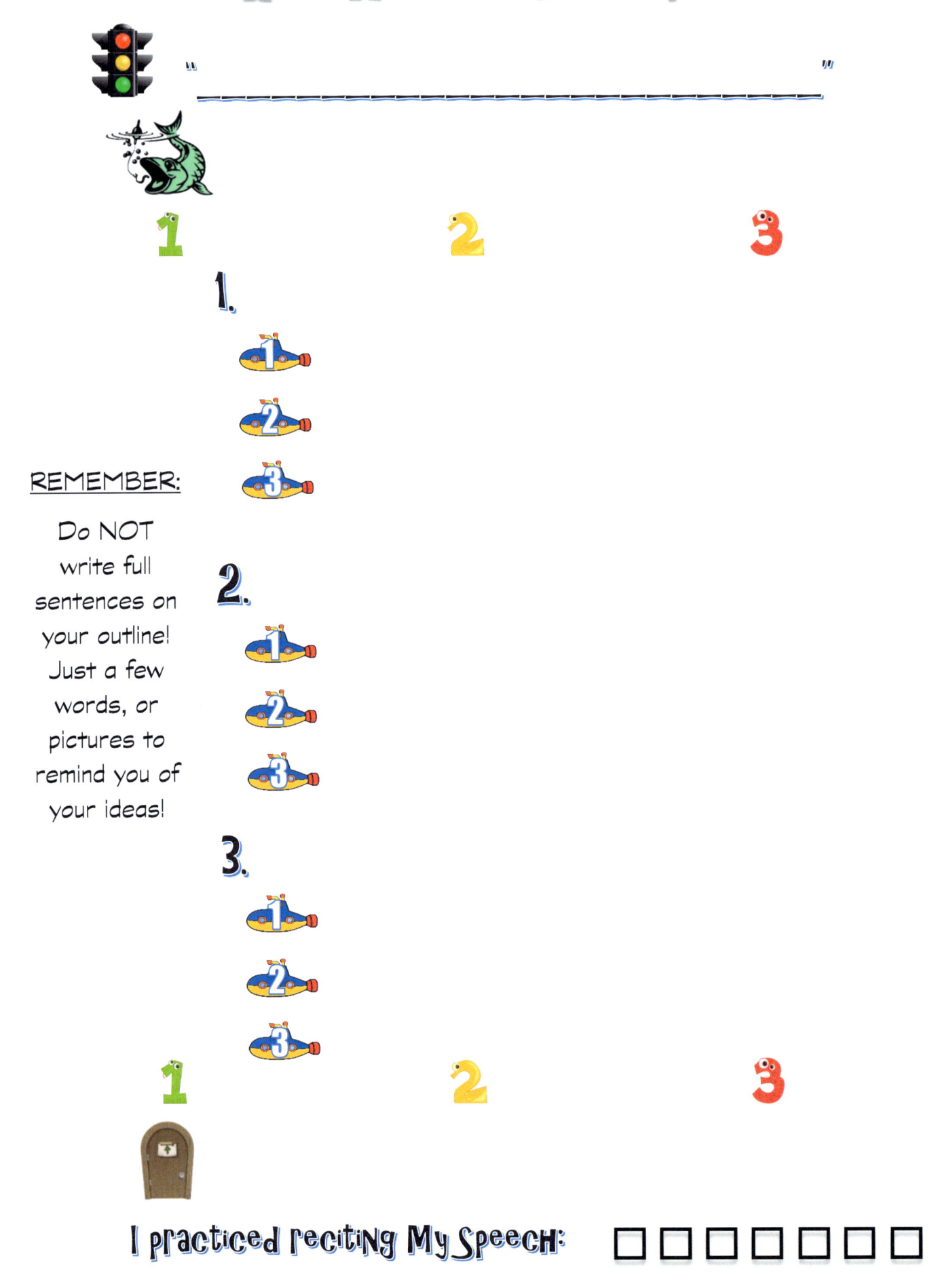

"_____"

      1   **2**   **3**

1.
- 1
- 2
- 3

REMEMBER:

Do NOT write full sentences on your outline! Just a few words, or pictures to remind you of your ideas!

2.
- 1
- 2
- 3

3.
- 1
- 2
- 3

      1   **2**   **3**

I practiced reciting my speech: ☐ ☐ ☐ ☐ ☐ ☐ ☐

Week 11 - Scorecard

Speech Writing Skills

Speech Delivery Skills

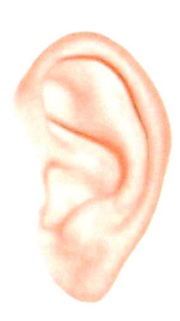

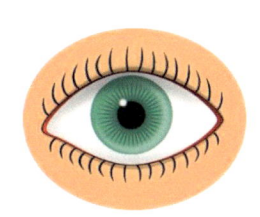

Circle **THREE** skills you did well.

Underline **TWO** items to work on next week.

My speech was persuasive!

I earned $_____

Week 12 - RoadMap

REVIEW YOUR SKILLS!

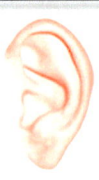

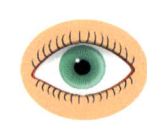

🚦 "_____"

1. _____
   🚤1 _____
   🚤2 _____
   🚤3 _____

2. _____
   🚤1 _____
   🚤2 _____
   🚤3 _____

3. _____
   🚤1 _____
   🚤2 _____
   🚤3 _____

Week 12 - Outline

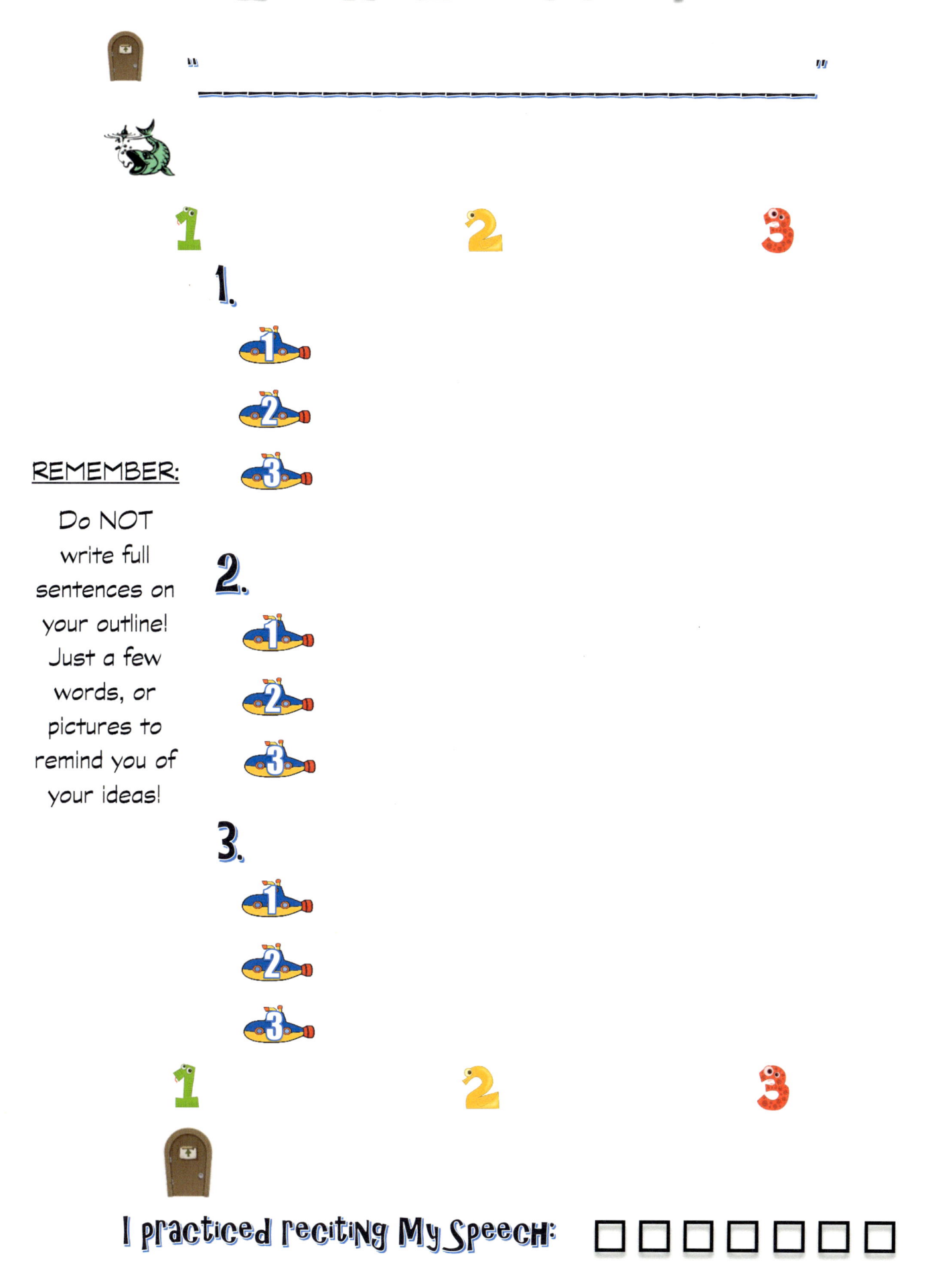

" _____ "

1 **2** **3**

1.

    ①

    ②

    ③

REMEMBER:

Do NOT write full sentences on your outline! Just a few words, or pictures to remind you of your ideas!

2.

    ①

    ②

    ③

3.

    ①

    ②

    ③

1 **2** **3**

I practiced reciting my speech: ☐ ☐ ☐ ☐ ☐ ☐ ☐

Week 12 - Scorecard

Speech Writing Skills

Speech Delivery Skills

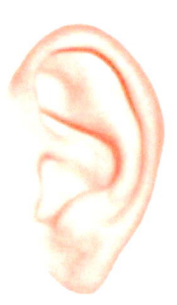

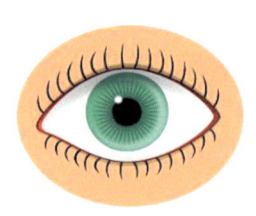

Circle **THREE** skills you did well.

Underline **TWO** items to work on next week.

My speech was persuasive!

I earned $_____

Week 13 – RoadMap (at home)

You Choose! Create a Speech of your choice this week! You will give your final speech to an adult friend or parent this week, and ask them to give you feedback by completing the "Super Scorecard". Instead of presenting prepared speeches, we will be working on impromptu speeches in class this week.

"_____"

1.
_____
1. _____
2. _____
3. _____

2.
_____
1. _____
2. _____
3. _____

3.
_____
1. _____
2. _____
3. _____

Week 13 - Outline (at home)

🚦 "_____"

🐟

1.
  🚤1
  🚤2
  🚤3

REMEMBER:
Do NOT write full sentences on your outline! Just a few words, or pictures to remind you of your ideas!

2.
  🚤1
  🚤2
  🚤3

3.
  🚤1
  🚤2
  🚤3

🚪

I practiced reciting my speech: ☐ ☐ ☐ ☐ ☐ ☐ ☐

Week 13 – Super Scorecard

Speech Writing Skills   Comments

🐟   1   2   3   4   5   _____

123   1   2   3   4   5   _____

🚪   1   2   3   4   5   _____

🚢   1   2   3   4   5   _____

Speech Delivery Skills   Comments

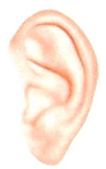

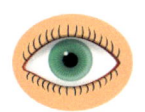

👂   1   2   3   4   5   _____

🌳   1   2   3   4   5   _____

👁   1   2   3   4   5   _____

👟   1   2   3   4   5   _____

Week 13 – (In Class) RoadMap

Use this worksheet to prepare your impromptu speech in class this week!

" _____ "

1   **2**   **3**

1.

2.

3.

1   **2**   **3**

Week 13 - Scorecard

Speech Writing Skills

Speech Delivery Skills

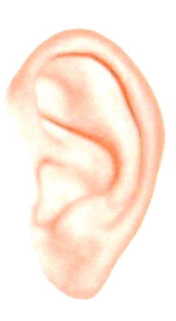

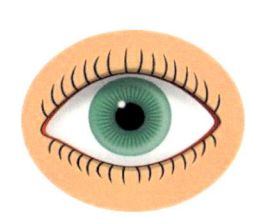

Circle THREE skills you did well.

Underline TWO items to work on next week.

Week 14 – Impromptu

Learning to give quality impromptu speeches will prepare you for many situations in life that require you to have a quick response. Impromptu speeches can sometimes be called "Limited Prep". In general, the speaker pulls a subject and has a few minutes to prepare a speech on that topic. This tests the speaker's ability to organize their ideas and think quickly. Use the Roadmap on the following page to practice quickly organizing your thoughts when given an impromptu topic. 3-5 minutes of prep time would be plenty. The list below has numerous ideas for Impromptu topics! Looking for more? Access more free impromptu topics and downloadable worksheets at bigbrainbuzz.com/publicspeakingfreebies

Impromptu Topics:

- The best surprise ever.
- If I were invisible for a day…
- How to impress your parents.
- How to spend a million dollars
- A day in my life.
- If I could travel through time.
- My favorite book.
- An important lesson I've learned.
- Three things I'd change if I ruled the world.
- How to make your favorite meal.
- The worst chores at home.
- Why I deserve an allowance.
- Why you need a baby brother or sister.
- How to annoy an older sister/brother.
- How to save money.
- Three things that scare me.
- How to spend a rainy day.
- How to walk a dog.
- Why your mom/dad is special.
- Great things about the ocean.
- Things I'll never eat.
- Why I like my town.
- The best parts of a parade.
- Why are manners important?
- If I were an animal, I would be…
- Things to remember when you're camping.
- What you'd find under my bed.
- When is lying a good idea?
- If I had a million dollars to give away.
- If I ruled the world…
- My favorite of the five senses
- Ways to help other people…
- If I could be really good at something, I would want it to be…
- If I had to live on a desert island, I would want to have these three things…
- Is it ok to lie?
- How to make a pizza
- Why holidays are important
- If I could only eat three foods forever.
- Why books are important.
- Is it right to keep animals in a zoo?
- Dogs are better than cats (or vice versa)
- Things you do well

Week 14 – RoadMap

Practice – IMPROMPTU:

Learning to give quality impromptu speeches will prepare you for many situations in life that require you to have a quick response. Use this worksheet to practice the art of quickly (3-5 minutes) outlining an organized topic list, hook and closing. You may want to make multiple copies of this page. Get free downloadable copies of these forms to practice a new impromptu speech every day this week at: **bigbrainbuzz.com/publicspeakingfreebies**

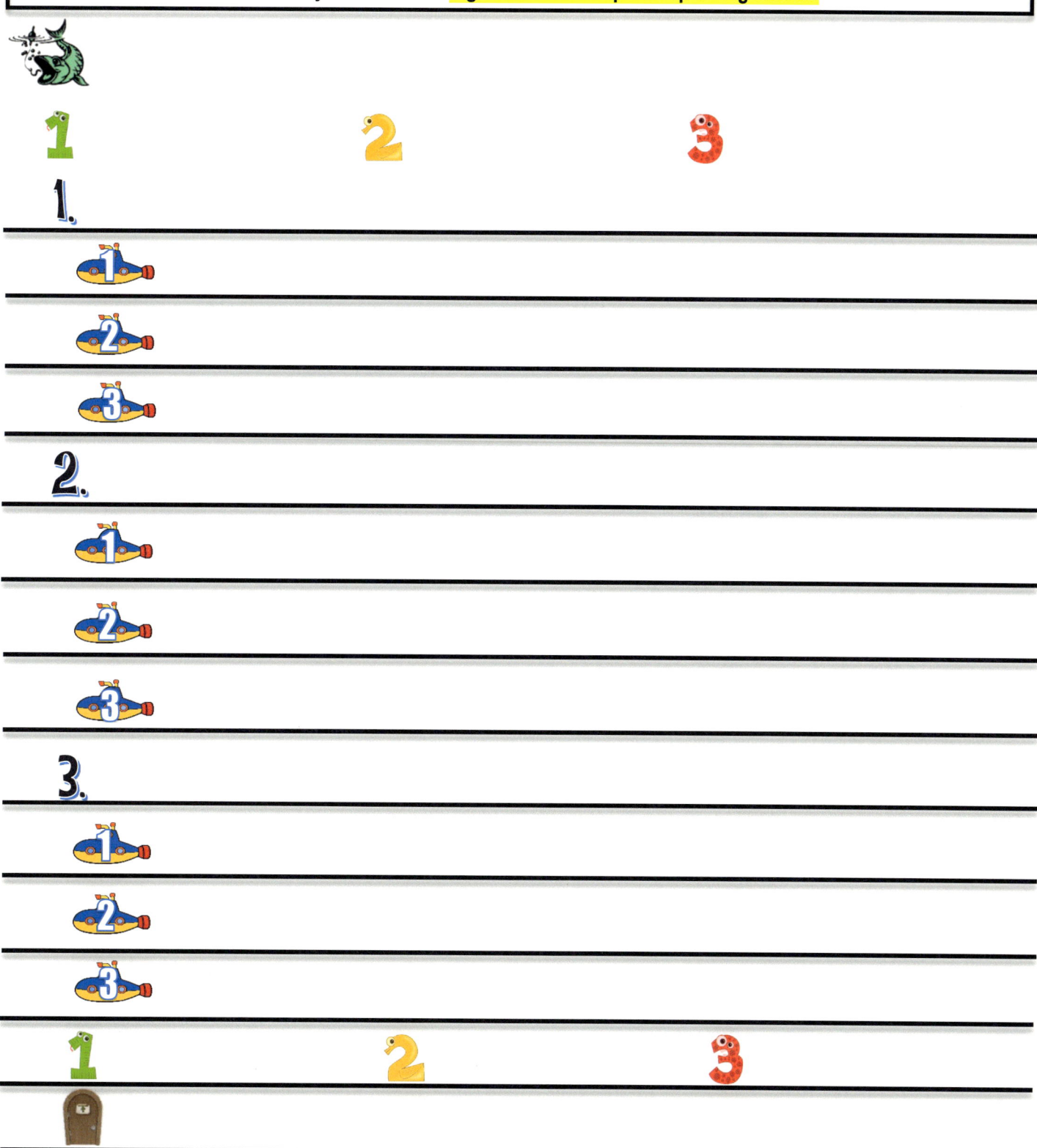

1 **2** **3**

1. _____

  🚤1 _____

  🚤2 _____

  🚤3 _____

2. _____

  🚤1 _____

  🚤2 _____

  🚤3 _____

3. _____

  🚤1 _____

  🚤2 _____

  🚤3 _____

1 **2** **3**

_____

Week 14 - Outline

_____

1.
  1.
  2.
  3.

TIPS FOR IMPROMPTU:

Decide on your 3 big ideas first. Then choose the three sub-topics under each idea. Next, decide on your hook. Last, create your closing that reflects the hook.

2.
  1.
  2.
  3.

3.
  1.
  2.
  3.

I practiced my speech: ☐ ☐ ☐ ☐ ☐ ☐

Week 14 – (In Class) RoadMap

Use this worksheet to prepare your impromptu speech in class this week!

"_____"

1 **2** **3**

1.
_____
🚤1 _____
🚤2 _____
🚤3 _____

2.
_____
🚤1 _____
🚤2 _____
🚤3 _____

3.
_____
🚤1 _____
🚤2 _____
🚤3 _____

1 **2** **3**
_____

Week 14 - Scorecard

Speech Writing Skills

Speech Delivery Skills

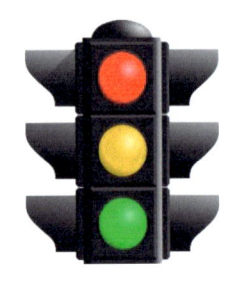

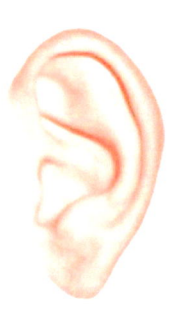

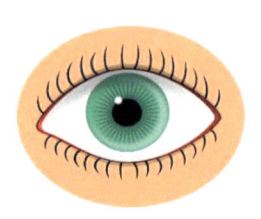

Circle THREE skills you did well.

Underline TWO items to work on next week.

Week 15 - RoadMap

NEW SKILL: <u>Visual Aids</u> add interest to your presentation. However, they can easily become a distraction if the presenter is not skilled in displaying and using them. We will spend the next few weeks practicing the art of using Visual Aids. Don't forget to use all of the skills you have learned this year!

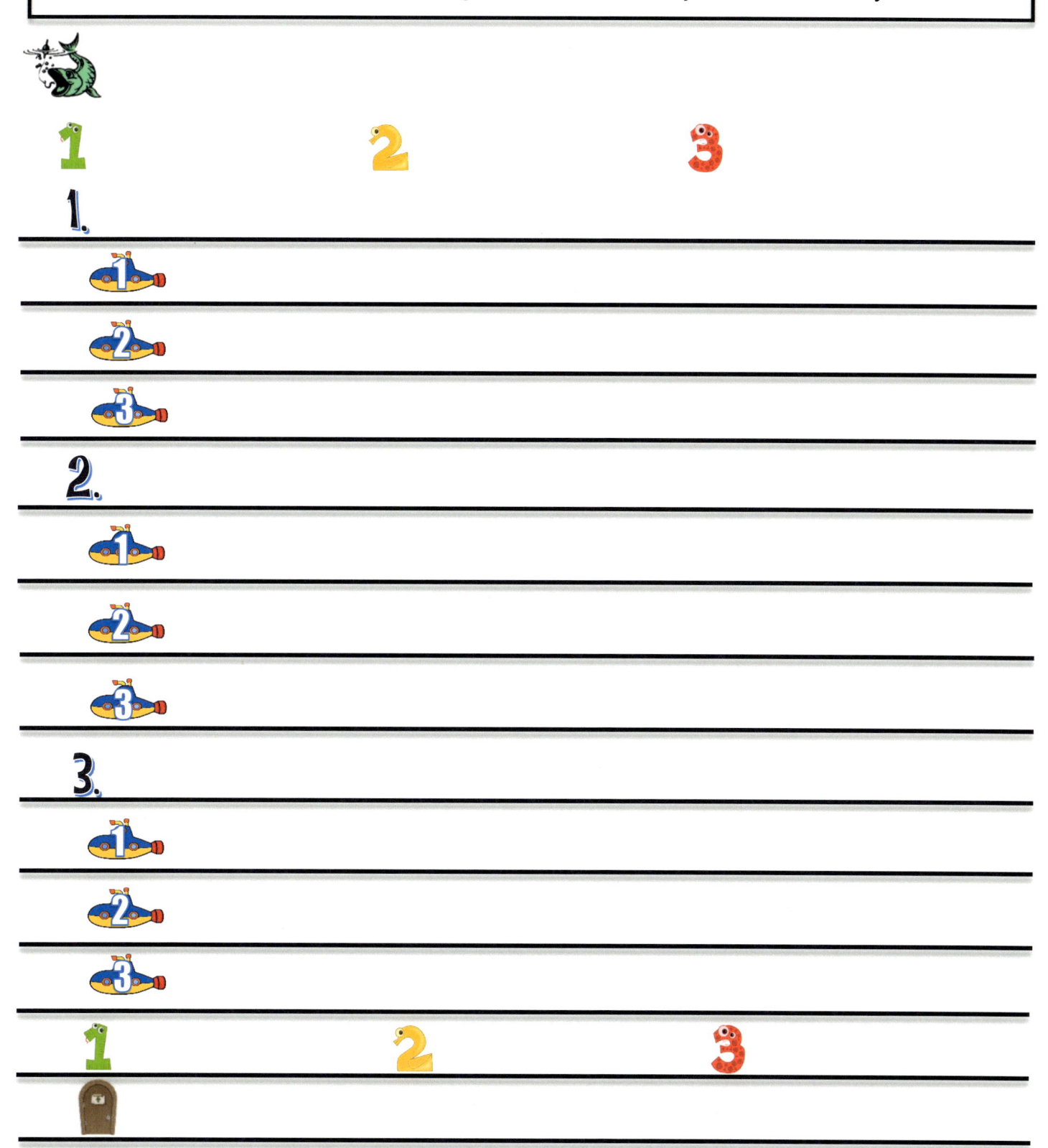

1 **2** **3**

1.
- 1.
- 2.
- 3.

2.
- 1.
- 2.
- 3.

3.
- 1.
- 2.
- 3.

1 **2** **3**

Week 15 - Outline

" _____ "

1.
   1.
   2.
   3.

2.
   1.
   2.
   3.

3.
   1.
   2.
   3.

PRACTICE USING YOUR VISUAL AID!

You may want to practice in front of a mirror. Experiment with different techniques to introduce and utilize your visual aid during your presentation.

I practiced my speech: ☐ ☐ ☐ ☐ ☐ ☐

Week 15 - Scorecard

Speech Writing Skills

Speech Delivery Skills

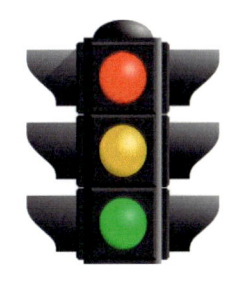

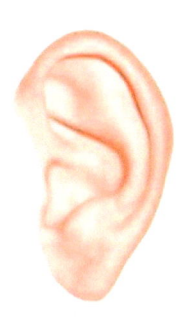

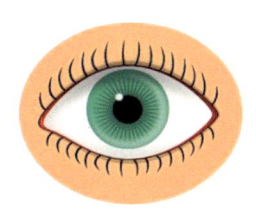

Circle **THREE** skills you did well.

Underline **TWO** items to work on next week.

Week 16 - RoadMap

New Style: **DEMONSTRATIONS:** This week, you will prepare a demonstration. These are fun speeches that teach the class how to do something! You will continue to practice the art of using visual aids by integrating them into your demonstration. Be sure to practice with them as you prepare for the upcoming week.

1   **2**   **3**

1. _____
   - 1 _____
   - 2 _____
   - 3 _____

2. _____
   - 1 _____
   - 2 _____
   - 3 _____

3. _____
   - 1 _____
   - 2 _____
   - 3 _____

1   **2**   **3**

Week 16 - Outline

"_____"

1.
 - 1
 - 2
 - 3

PRACTICE USING YOUR VISUAL AID!

You may want to practice in front of a mirror. Experiment with different techniques to introduce and utilize your visual aid during your presentation.

2.
 - 1
 - 2
 - 3

3.
 - 1
 - 2
 - 3

I practiced my speech: ☐ ☐ ☐ ☐ ☐ ☐

Week 16 - Scorecard

Speech Writing Skills

Speech Delivery Skills

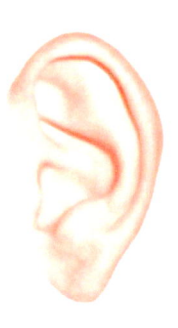

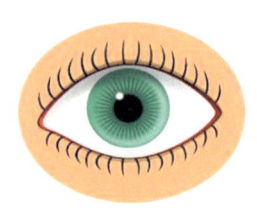

Circle THREE skills you did well.

Underline TWO items to work on next week.

Week 17 - RoadMap

New Style: <u>INTERPRETATION:</u> This type of presentation is sometimes called "Oratorical" and can be really fun because they require creativity. You will need to use skills similar to what an actor might use to pretend to be a character, or to get your audience to feel or believe something.

New Skill: Characterization

Penguin Pirate reminds us that we need to act out the characters in our interpretive presentations! In order for the audience to believe we are a pirate, we need to think about how a pirate might act.

The goal is to act out the character so well that everyone in the audience knows exactly what type of character you are. We will use this picture of <u>Penguin Pirate</u> to remind us of characterization. This penguin wants us to believe he is a pirate. He might say something like "aye matey", "walk the plank", "arrrrrr", "shiver me timbers", etc.) He might pretend he is wearing an eye patch, or pretend there is a parrot on his shoulder. Maybe he closes his fist and lifts his arm forward to make us believe he is holding a sword. You will need to think about the characters in your story and make us feel like they are in the room with us!

Because this technique requires more skill and feedback to do it well, we will be working on the <u>SAME poem or short story for 3 weeks</u>, and improving it each week. Each week we will add a new interpretation skill, so be sure to pick a poem or short story that you want to keep working on. Also, you will want to select something that is a very simple story like The Three Little Pigs, or Little Red Riding Hood, if this is your first attempt at an interpretive speech. For more poem or short story ideas, and other bonus material, go to: **bigbrainbuzz.com/publicspeakingfreebies**

<u>THIS WEEK, we will focus primarily on our VOICES.</u> Practice reciting your short story or poem using a voice technique that makes up understand who your character is. Do they have an accent? Are they a young child that might need a sweeter, higher-pitched voice? Or are they older and need a deeper voice? Are they male or female? Would they generally speak boldly and loudly, or delicate and soft?

<u>NOTE:</u> You may have to cut out small pieces of the story to keep within the time limit. You may also choose to remove a character if there are too many in the story to act out well. Cut out sections here or there, but be sure to keep the most important parts.

Week 17 – RoadMap
(continued)

Paste a copy of your story below:

After selecting your short story or poem, you will want to re-write it and remove any sections that you aren't planning to present. You can either paste a handwritten page, or typed version below:

I practiced My Speech: ☐ ☐ ☐ ☐ ☐ ☐ ☐ ☐ ☐ ☐ ☐ ☐

Week 17 - Scorecard

Speech Delivery Skills

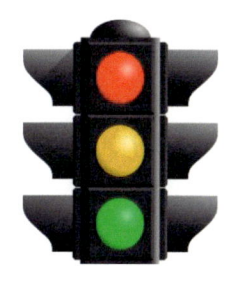

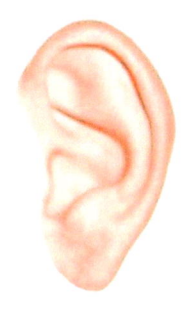

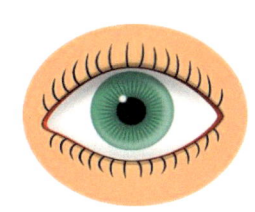

Circle **TWO** skills you did well.

Underline **ONE** item to work on next week.

Characterization:

I Could Improve My Characterization By:

_____

Voices: _____

_____

_____

Week 18 – RoadMap

NEW SKILL:

GESTURES: This week, as we work on our speeches, we will focus on the use of gestures – moving our body in a way that brings the characters to life. Do the characters stand tall and proud? Do they slouch and cross their arms? Are they angry or irritated with their hands on their hips? Are their arms waving around or are they hanging by their side? Are they holding an imaginary item like a sword or a book? How do you think they would be acting? We will use this picture of "Red Bird" to remember to use gestures. See how he is using his wings to tell us something?

To practice this skill, it may be useful to give your speech in front of a mirror. You should also practice plenty of times in front of parents or siblings. They will be able to offer more ideas to make your character believable.

Some ideas for gestures in my speech are:

_____

_____

_____

_____

_____

_____

_____

I practiced my speech: ☐ ☐ ☐ ☐ ☐ ☐ ☐ ☐ ☐ ☐

Week 18 - Scorecard

Speech Delivery Skills

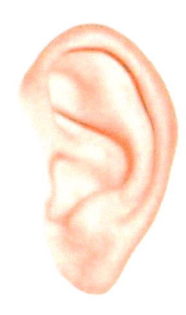

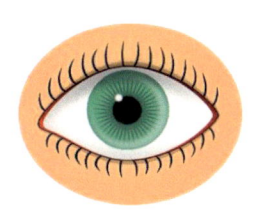

Circle **TWO** skills you did well.

Underline **ONE** item to work on next week.

Characterization:

I could Improve My Characterization By:

Voices:
_____
_____

Gestures:
_____
_____
_____

Week 19 – RoadMap

New Skill: Memorization

MEMORY MAN: An interpretive speech really requires complete memorization. In order to really get the audience to understand your character, and to use your voice and gestures well, you have to memorize it word-for-word. Memorization is such a great skill to have. When we see "Memory Man", we remember to work hard to memorize our speeches. There are a few things that can help make memorization easier…..

1. Repetition – just practicing over and over again will help you naturally memorize the material.
2. You can still use an outline for the key parts of the story, but remember to stick to the same words each time. You may also draw faces or stick-figures on your outline to remind you of a special voice or gesture you were planning to use. Over time, try to present your speech without using the outline and only refer to it in a pinch.
3. Practice in front of the mirror and other people. Many times, it seems easy to remember your speech until you get in front of someone – then your memory goes out the window!!! Practice delivering your speech in front of others from the beginning, and it will help you identify parts that you might not have memorized as well.
4. If you always forget a line at the same place every time, think of a way to tie the two lines together. Is there a picture you can think of in your head that will help remind you of the next line?
5. Be careful not to sound like a robot. Sometimes when we recite something word-for-word, the audience can tell we are thinking of each sentence in our head. We don't want them to pay attention to the fact that we have something memorized. We want them to pay attention to our interesting voices and gestures. As you practice, this will become easier.

I Practiced My Speech:

Day 1: ☐ ☐ ☐ ☐ ☐

Day 2: ☐ ☐ ☐ ☐ ☐

Day 3: ☐ ☐ ☐ ☐ ☐

Day 4: ☐ ☐ ☐ ☐ ☐

Week 20 - RoadMap

INTERPRETATION:

Improving Skills by Practicing Famous Speeches

FAMOUS SPEECHES:

Over the next four weeks, we will refine our speaking skills by studying and presenting famous speeches from history. You are not creating your own speech, but memorizing and delivering someone else's speech. The goal is to mimic a master. If you are brand new to this type of speech, it may be easier to use a speech that has a video of the speaker delivering it. That way, you can practice some of their tone, gestures, etc. If it is only a written copy (perhaps it was before the TV was invented or it was not recorded), you will have more freedom to try to guess how the original speaker may have presented the material.

Time Limit: You must also keep in mind you will need to recite it in the 3-minute time frame, so you may have to select just a portion of the speech to deliver. Be careful not to trim sections in a way that changes the speaker's original intent.

Choose Carefully: You will want to choose your speech carefully, since you will be working on it for many weeks, and will not be able to change it after this week. It is ok if other students in the class have the same speech.

New Skill: Tempo

As we get even better at delivering speeches, we can start to add in a change of tempo to help make things exciting. You can have a dramatic pause, where the audience is waiting for more. You could speak a sentence quickly, increasing your volume, then slow it down and get a bit quieter. We will use the picture of the race car to remind us to adjust our tempo. When the race car goes around a corner, they must adjust their speed to make the best turn. Sometimes they are driving as fast as they can, other times they are more controlled and slow-down in order to stay on course. As you recite your speech this week, find opportunities to adjust your tempo for dramatic effect.

One person who used tempo to his advantage was Martin Luther King Jr. Here is a short video clip of his famous "I Have a Dream" speech. Pay special attention to his tempo: (Play THIS VIDEO – 1.5 minutes)

Week 20 - RoadMap
(continued)

Famous Speech Ideas:

Select from the list below, or find a new one!

For more famous speech ideas, and bonus material, go to:
bigbrainbuzz.com/publicspeakingfreebies

- Abraham Lincoln – "The Gettysburg Address"
- Winston Churchill – "We Shall Fight On the Beaches"
- Susan B. Anthony - "After Being Convicted Of Voting In The 1872 Presidential Election"
- Martin Luther King Jr – "I have a Dream"
- Elizabeth I – "Speech to the Troops"
- John F. Kennedy – "The Decision to Go To The Moon"

I practiced My Speech:

Day 1: ☐ ☐ ☐ ☐ ☐

Day 2: ☐ ☐ ☐ ☐ ☐

Day 3: ☐ ☐ ☐ ☐ ☐

Day 4: ☐ ☐ ☐ ☐ ☐

Week 20 – RoadMap
(continued)

Paste a copy of your Famous Speech Below:

After selecting your famous speech, you may want to trim sections to remain within the three-minute time limit. You can either paste a handwritten page, or typed version below. After practicing for a few days, break the speech into small sections and create notecards with key words and/or pictures to guide you through your speech.

Week 20 - Scorecard

Speech Delivery Skills

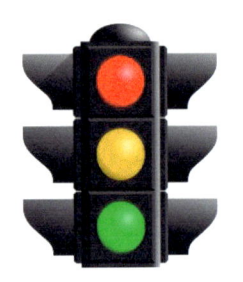

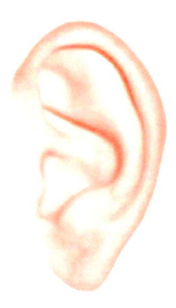

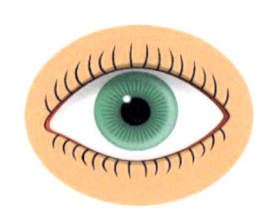

🚦 👂 🌳 👁 👟

Circle TWO skills you did well.
Underline ONE item to work on next week.

Tempo:
I should speak faster or slower for emphasis in these sections:

_____
_____
_____
_____

Week 21 - RoadMap

USING NOTECARDS:

This week, you will be transferring your speech to notecards.

REMEMBER these guidelines:

1. Your first notecard will include a brief background about the speech as an introduction.
    a. **Example:** "When Martin Luther King Jr. delivered his "I Have a Dream" speech, before a crowd of 250,000 people at the 1963 March on Washington, it became one of the most famous speeches in history. I would like to share a portion of it with you today."
2. The remaining notecards are for the content of your speech. **DO NOT WRITE THE ENTIRE SPEECH ON THE NOTECARDS!**
    a. First, use the Outline on the following page to summarize the parts of the speech into sections using key words or pictures to remind you of the content of the speech.
    b. AFTER you have used your outline page, transfer the summarized material to a notecard.
3. PRACTICE using the notecards to give your speech.
    a. If you stumble in a section, modify the notecard to offer more help.
    b. Be careful not to fidget with the notecards. Don't roll them, wave them, etc.
    c. Reminder: By the end of this course, you will deliver this speech without your notecards.

I practiced My Speech:

Day 1: ☐ ☐ ☐ ☐ ☐

Day 2: ☐ ☐ ☐ ☐ ☐

Day 3: ☐ ☐ ☐ ☐ ☐

Day 4: ☐ ☐ ☐ ☐ ☐

Week 21 - Outline

"_____"

Background Information:

-
-
-
-
-
-
-
-
-
-
-
-
-

Week 21 - Scorecard

Speech Delivery Skills

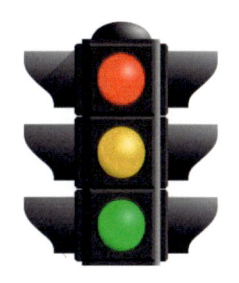

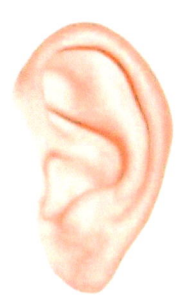

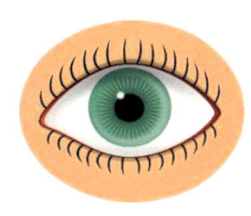

Circle TWO skills you did well.

Underline ONE item to work on next week.

Suggestions from Classmates or Parents::

_____

_____

_____

_____

Week 22 - RoadMap

New Skill: Volume

Last week we adjusted our tempo at various times in our speech to add emphasis. This week, we will adjust the volume of our voice to add emphasis. When we speak loudly, people notice! But did you know they also notice when we intentionally speak softly? Speaking softly requires the audience to listen closely.

This week, look at the different parts of your speech and identify sections where you might want to adjust your volume. Remember, volume is used to bring attention to what we are saying, and to help the audience pay attention. The majority of your speech will be given at an average volume. Key points will be adjusted louder or softer depending on the type of impact you want. Two things to consider:

- Speaking Loud usually "shocks" or "confronts" the audience.
- Speaking softly usually emphasizes a more personal mood – something they should ponder

I practiced My Speech:

Day 1: ☐ ☐ ☐ ☐ ☐

Day 2: ☐ ☐ ☐ ☐ ☐

Day 3: ☐ ☐ ☐ ☐ ☐

Day 4: ☐ ☐ ☐ ☐ ☐

Week 22 - Scorecard

Speech Delivery Skills

Circle TWO skills you did well.

Underline ONE item to work on next week.

Suggestions from classmates or parents::

_____

_____

_____

_____

Week 23 - RoadMap

Gestures & Positioning

Last time we talked about gestures, we were pretending to be a character in our short stories. This time, we will use gestures differently.

In formal speeches like the ones we have been working on, a speaker generally uses three main gestures: intentional steps, moving the arms at specific points, and using the head to focus on various sections of the audience. If the speaker is not using a podium, they will take intentional steps. They may take one diagonal step to the right and speak for a while, then step sideways to the center and speak for a while, then sideways again to the left. After their last big idea, they may step diagonally backwards and to the center for their final thoughts. This type of movement creates an outline for the audience to hang the information on. They get the sense that the speech has a beginning, middle and end. It makes the speech more interesting and engages the audience better than standing in one place.

The speaker will many time use their arms and hands to emphasize a portion of the speech. You will want to think carefully about your arm movements. You may decide to pound on the podium for a dramatic point, or pound a fist against your chest. You may just space your arms out diagonally in front of you and signal that what you are saying is one of your big ideas.

With a parent, watch some videos online this week to observe various arm gestures in speeches. Then, choose the ones that best fit your speech and practice using them in front of a mirror.

I practiced My Speech:

Day 1: ☐ ☐ ☐ ☐ ☐

Day 2: ☐ ☐ ☐ ☐ ☐

Day 3: ☐ ☐ ☐ ☐ ☐

Day 4: ☐ ☐ ☐ ☐ ☐

Week 23 - Scorecard

Speech Delivery Skills

Circle **TWO** skills you did well.

Underline **ONE** item to work on next week.

Suggestions from classmates or parents::

___
___
___
___

Week 24 - RoadMap

THE FINAL STRETCH!!!

Can you believe this is our last week? You will focus on polishing your speech, in preparation for a larger audience at the end of the week.

New: Appearance

Whether we like it or not, most people will decide if you are someone worth listening to before you even open your mouth! That is because the way we dress and present ourselves communicates to people just like our words do. When we have not combed our hair or brushed our teeth, it tells people that we don't care about keeping our bodies healthy. When we dress in dirty or wrinkled clothes, or clothes meant for play time, it is hard for others to take us seriously.

If we want people to pay attention to our words, we have to make sure we are not distracting them with poor hygiene and sloppy clothing. Instead, we present ourselves with authority on our toic by dressing in clean, well-fitting clothes that communicate a level of professionalism. Many times, for famous speeches that might mean a button-down shirt with a tie and slacks for boy. Girls may wear a professional-looking dress or a nice shirt and pants with closed-toes shoes. These are suggestions. Consider your speech and what you think would be appropriate. Depending on your topic, you may want to dress in a clothing that would be relevant to that time period. You decide what will give the audience the best chance to hear your words and remember your ideas.

I practiced My Speech:

Day 1: ☐ ☐ ☐ ☐ ☐

Day 2: ☐ ☐ ☐ ☐ ☐

Day 3: ☐ ☐ ☐ ☐ ☐

Day 4: ☐ ☐ ☐ ☐ ☐

Congratulations!!!

You have completed "Public Speaking For Kids - Level One"!

Think about what great progress you have made this year!

We would love to see a speech you gave at the beginning of the year and compare it to your final speech!

Upload them to the Big Brain Buzz - Public Speaking Group Facebook page to share your progress!

Check out "Public Speaking For Kids - Level 2" to continue your progress!

Find us at http://www.bigbrainbuzz.com!